CW00369133

# OVER 100 TRIPLE X SEX TRICKS

THIS IS A CARLTON BOOK

Text and design copyright © Carlton Books Limited 2005

This edition published by
Carlton Books Limited 2005
20 Mortimer Street
London W1T 3JW

A CIP catalogue record for this book is available from the British Library.

ISBN 1 84442 480 4

Printed and bound in Singapore

Executive Editor: Lisa Dyer
Cover: Karin Fremer
Design: Michelle Pickering
Copy Editor: Gillian Holmes
Production Controller: Caroline Alberti

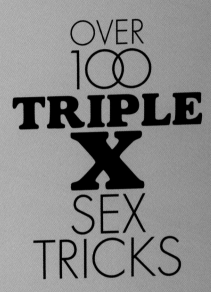

# COSMOPOLITAN

## OVER 100 TRIPLE X SEX TRICKS

### LISA SUSSMAN

CARLTON
BOOKS

# Section One

## Thrill Level

When appropriate, text is rated to determine the Triple X level as follows:

**S:** Steam it up

**E:** Edgy and Wild

**X:** Extreme Kink

# Max Out Your Pleasure

Even good sex can become routine. Your body may wobble every time, but it's more because you're using tried-and-tested methods than making a buzz with erotic energy. The good news is that it's easy to add a jolt to routine sex. Just take a stroll on the wild side.

Doing something you've never done before can send your system into overdrive. When you go beyond your limits, you discover hidden turn-ons and new sensations – maybe even a hot zone you never knew you had. Plus, you get the blood-pumping high that comes from being bolder in bed. Your willingness to explore your sexual boundaries will help build intimacy and trust between you and your partner.

When you think about it … is there any reason *not* to have a naughty day?

# Pillow Talk

Truly amazing erotic action can happen only when both partners are willing to take risks. Here are eight steps to calm your lover's fears and to get them involved in your secret desires (and liking it!) without setting off perv alarms.

1
Don't beg. Don't grovel. It's not seemly. And it's not necessary. Your best move: Give the relationship a month or two before **breaking out the vibe**.

2
Make sure they know they can **melt you down** sans kink.

3
A weekend away is a good time to get the ball rolling. A **change of scenery** makes people more open to new things.

When the time comes, don't jump right in and unload. Here are four strategies for talking yourself into a wilder sex life, depending on your personality type.

- **If you're shy:** Don't bother talking. Instead, slyly test the waters – see how they react to doing something slightly off from your usual routine. Get into a new position or hold their wrists down. If they act unruffled, they're probably open to at least listening to the idea of doing something a bit unusual. **S**

- **If you're too embarrassed:** Blame it on Freud. Say you had a dream and then describe in detail your favourite wild fantasy. If they're aroused, they'll ask if you want to make it a reality. **E**

- **If you're bold:** Ask about the best sex they've ever had. Or their favourite fantasy. Discovering what they like instead of barking out your wants will make your partner feel less intimidated. Hopefully, if they're half the lover you think they are, they will start asking what *you* like, too. After you tell them, you can show them. **E**

- **If you're a risk taker:** Offer to be their sex slave for the entire day. **X**

Simplify by using a visual aid. You can get a **video or book** with a scene that illustrates your deepest desire. The key, though, is to be specific – 'Do you see that? That makes me really hot.' You can't just watch the film or look at the book and hope they magically get it. **S**

Take a leaf from the *Kama Sutra*. Breaching carnal taboos doesn't sound freaky when it reads like poetry. Instead of asking your lover if they want to try it up the bum, ask if they'd enjoy '**flower congress**'. And rather than wondering if your lover is into light spanking, enquire if they'd like to make the sound 'Hin'. Doesn't that sound much better? **S**

Be prepared for the need for some **damage control**. If you went too far, too fast, here's some phrases to memorize to keep them from running into the night.

- Sorry, you just looked so hot lying/bending/bouncing like that, I couldn't resist.
- I've never had anyone do that with me before, and I wanted to know what it would be like. You're the first person I've felt comfortable enough to ask.
- Just kidding!
- I thought we could have a naughty little secret between the two of us.

Quit while you're ahead. If they flinched when you climbed on top, it's probably not a great idea to break out the fuzzy cuffs. But even if this isn't for them, maybe they'll like the **flavoured massage oil**.

# Rules of the Game

Erotic extras spice up the bedroom, but they can also backfire. Beware of these passion poopers (all players must read the following before starting).

**9**

Heating it up:
Nuking marshmallows,
chocolate sauce or honey and
**dripping it over each other's body**
sounds like a sweet idea, but the results
can actually be *too* hot for lovers and cause
surface skin burns (same goes for candle
wax). Stay in lukewarm territory (if you
can dip your finger in without agony,
it's probably okay).

Beware **alien invasions**: Don't use
any object that's not specifically
designed for that part of the body –
inserting certain fruit and veggies (see
next tip for the exceptions), cooking tools
and **candles in the vagina** for instance. But also
anal vibrators in the vagina, rubber bands around
the penis and so on. You can cause an irritation
at the very least and serious injury in a worst-case
scenario (do you really want to explain how the
vacuum cleaner nozzle got stuck up your bottom?).

Eat your fruit and vegetables: As long as you don't use any food that can break off or get stuck in the vaginal canal, **inserting food** is no more dangerous than inserting a dildo. Things that potentially will not come out are off limits (like grapes). Avoid spicy foods because they could burn. If you use sweet foods near your vaginal area, wash well afterwards to prevent yeast infections. Anything with oil in it (such as chocolate or whipped cream) can burn holes in latex birth control.

Check what's in your **lube**. Some aren't safe to use with latex, others will harm silicone toys.

Don't be a blow-hard: If air is blown directly into the vagina during oral sex, there's a risk it'll accidentally create an air embolus – an **air bubble** that blocks the passage of blood in an artery or vein – which could have lethal consequences.

14

Say what you mean and mean what you say. If you tell your lover, **'I just want to tie up your hands'** and as soon as they oblige, you fasten their feet too, they'll never play cops and robbers with you again – you messed with their trust.

**15** Before starting, make sure you're **packing the right tools**. Like if they've agreed to let you go knockin' at the back door, have lube ready and waiting. Or if you're filming your action, make sure the camera is charged up.

Only the brave (and probably not too bright) would let a partner render them helpless after a few dates. **Know your partner** before getting tied up. And never divulge personal info to a cyber-buddy.

Before trying anything new, make a **code word** to stop play. This way, if your lover does something too freaky, you can alert them – IMMEDIATELY. Especially if you're all tied up. Make it an attention-grabber like 'Vinegar'. 'Stop' doesn't work because they may think it's of the 'Stop, it feels so good' variety, as opposed to 'I want everything to stop NOW, no more games, scene over, let me outta here!'

Ignore pain at your peril. Sure, sometimes getting kinky is about upping the **fear factor**. But if that clamp is turning their extremities blue, don't ruin the moment by forcing them to go on. If spanking is part of your play, keep away from kidneys, liver, spleen or tailbone.

**18 18 18 18 18**

**19 19 19**

When tying things up, **keep it loose** – circulation is a good thing, especially in all the right parts. Tight scarves and handcuffs can cause numbness; blocking the nose or mouth can make you hyperventilate or induce a panic attack. And never tie anything around the neck. It's also good to have scissors on hand in case Mother shows up unannounced.

Everyone likes sex, but you should never be willing to die for it. HIV and AIDS are more easily spread through anal sex than any other sexual act, so always wear a condom when entering through the back door. Another **rule of the rear** is never to let him double-dip from bottom to vagina without re-rubbering up.

**Wash all toys** according to manufacturer's recommendations – it'll extend the life of your playthings as well as keep you infection-free.

# Bust Out of Your Sex Rut

Five really easy things to get you started on the path to the wild side – and no, you won't need any special equipment.*

**22**

Buy some **PVC, leather or suede**. Start small with a glove or a bit of material that you can lie on, wear or rub between your legs or anywhere else that takes your fancy when you make love.

*These all have a guaranteed **S** rating.

Hardcore players use slings purposely designed for some wild fun but you can get the same sensation with a cheap **hammock**. Hang it in a corner of your lounge so it looks like an innocent design feature. Then get **down and dirty** when the lights are out.

**TIP:** Lying-down hammock sex will just make you feel seasick. Instead, he should stand on the edge while you do **position gymnastics**.

Wrap a silk scarf around your hand. Rub it all over your lover's body, especially back and forth between the thighs and against the crotch. Tie it around his **nuts and bolts**, then tie a large knot with about 30 cm (12 in) of fabric on either end to hold onto. As you ride him, pull on the free ends so that the knot rubs against your love button while constricting his penis and scrotum (which can cause a harder erection). Yee-high!

2 4

Give your guy a demo of **how you touch yourself** when he's not around (it's a No. 1 male secret desire). Start coy with panties on, flicking your fingers through the soft, silky fabric. Payoff one: He'll learn exactly how to press your buttons. Payoff two: You will be the reigning queen in all his future fantasies.

**25**

**TIP:** To feel less like a solo act, include him – he can caress your other parts or he can give you his hand and you can use it how you like, making you queen for the day.

Attach a mirror to the ceiling above your bed for some voyeuristic fun.

**26**

# Section Two

# What to Wear, What to Wear

What makes on-the-edge clothes feel so extra-special sexy is that you can literally wear them anywhere. There is definitely a supermodel-thin line between what is high fashion and what is something you would find in a porn video – corsets, leather trousers, silky sheer shirts, lacy camisoles, fishnet stockings, PVC skirts and stilettos are just a few examples that have shown up on both sides of the style street.

All of which makes stocking up on your wardrobe a no-sweat, no-angst way to stretch your sexual boundaries. Read on for how to dress up your life.

# Seven-Day Sinner

Put this on your daily agenda: Seven days of dressing up a sexy, sultry you.

## MONDAY

AKA Moon Day. Wear white to work – but make it **secretive, sexy, lacy white**. Slip on a sheer white lace thong, a garter belt and a slinky barely-there white camisole under your usual work uniform; you'll feel like the drop-dead-gorgeous lunar goddess you really are! **S**

## TUESDAY

This is your inner-tramp day. Do something naughty that you always fantasized about, but your shy side got in the way. Leave the panties at home. Instead, wear **head-to-toe leather** or PVC. If your workplace shuns the Harley-Davidson look, slip on a leather thong and bra or 'jumper bumpers' – small metal rings that fit around your nipple to keep them erect. **E**

## WEDNESDAY

Mid-week – time to shake off stress, blahs and blues. In short, get a makeover. Hit a salon that can **give your downlow region a new look**. Hot pink dusted with glitter, royal blue with a white trim and lime green are just a few colours to dye for. If you can't get it done professionally, DIY with coloured mousse, gel or hair mascara that washes out with one shampoo (see tips 42–6 for more below-the-belt beauty tricks). **X**

## THURSDAY

The week is almost over, so what's a girl to do? Go shoe shopping. Find yourself the maddest, baddest **sky-high stilettos** you can. That extra six inches of height will transform you into a bona-fide dominatrix. To really get the kinks out, make them thigh-high and rubber. Now sashay your hot new self down the street. **X**

31

## FRIDAY

The day of dressing sex-cess. Start the day in red – teddy, camisole, panties and/or bra. Then slip on a silk or velvet shirt that comes off with a quick flick of the wrist (velcro-tabbed or via snaps). After hours, pull out the stops – with cleavage down to here and a long strand of beads dangling in between. Later, just wear the baubles. As things heat up, use them to **tease and please** your lucky lad, running them across his skin and wrapping them around his limbs. Then roll them into a ball and knead his body into a state of bliss. **S**

## SATURDAY

Get your booty shaking
by giving him a lap dance.
Do like the professionals
do: Keep your guy fully
clothed and make sure
you're only wearing
a G-string and heels.
Absolutely forbid him
to touch you (although
you can touch him) – it'll
give you a sexy, powerful
feeling, and seeing your
naked body but not being
able to touch will make
him crazed with desire.
Straddle his legs, and
wiggle your bottom.
**Grind slowly and
seductively** to the music,
stroking your breasts, and
making eye contact. Then
mambo your way over to
the mattress. **E**

## SUNDAY

Pour yourself into a sexy
silky negligee and refuse
to take it off (think of it
as the reverse strip). He
has to **kiss and lick** you
through the fabric. **S**

# Stripped Bare

It's not just what you wear – it's how you take it off. The last thing on his mind will be your cellulite. Promise!

34

Opt for an outfit that accentuates your assets. For example, if your breasts are best, wear a **cleavage-catapulting bustier**. For bottom babes, go for a bum-revealing G-string. **S**

So you don't **pop out** and knock him on the noggin, slowly **slip down** one bra strap and then the other before undoing your bra. **S**

**TIP:** Dangle the bra in front of him before dropping it on his lap.

Keep your heels on 'til the last minute. They'll lengthen your legs and make 'em look like something that's just strolled out of a **porn flick**. **E**

**37**

Wear stockings. You can give him a triple X view by sitting on a chair and lifting one leg at a time, then rolling the stocking s-l-o-w-l-y down with your palms. He'll be **howling oo-la-la**. E

Drape yourself with **feathery boas or silky scarves** that you can slide off later in the show. E

**38**

**3**

Avoid these fashion don'ts when stripping:

- **Tricky sleeve cuffs** – undo them first so you don't have to stop when slipping your shirt off
- **Tight-necked tops** – you don't want to get stuck mid-strip looking more like a turtle than eye candy
- **Elasticated waistbands** leave very unsexy marks on the skin
- **Back-fastening bras** – front closers avoid any passion-killing fumbling
- **Skip the suspenders** (garters) – lace hold-ups are much less fiddly.

**9**

**4**

Try switch-hitting by **stripping him**. Slowly undo his shirt. Gently slide it off, kissing and licking his chest. Get down on your knees and remove his shoes and socks. Fondle his penis through his pants as you slip them off. He'll be putty in your hands. **E**

# Hair Today, Gone Tomorrow

Tips for sexy head-to-crotch tresses.

**Wig out.** Try frolicking in the wig section of a department store. The payback for slipping on a totally new, man-made 'do? You can put on a different persona without much effort. Although you may, of course, need a fresh wardrobe to go with your **sexy new alter ego**. E

Dare to bare. Skip the usual bikini line trim and take it all off. Having nothing to cover you and buffer the sensation makes that area hypersensitive. And he'll love the **fuzz-free access** (Translation: More south-of-the-border mouth action for you). **X**

The best way to **go hairless** is to take a trip to your local waxing salon and let the professionals handle it. You can turn your expedition into a romp by taking him along. Some places even let him do the honours and **pull the wax**. Yeow – but at least he'll have an idea of what you're going through in the name of eroticism. **X**

44

If you opt to do it at home, turn it into a steamy love session. Light candles, prop yourself on the sink and **spread your legs wide**. He should take his own sweet time applying shaving cream. As he shaves you clean, he can slip in some teasing moves while whispering in a low, sexy voice how he's going to give you the best oral sex of your life. **X**

**TIP:** Old-fashioned switch-blades and disposable razors will give you nicks and burns. Use a safety razor, designed for female use.

Get creative and landscape your garden. Trim your hair into any pattern your heart desires: your boyfriend's initials, a lightning bolt, a butterfly – even an **arrow pointing down** (for the benefit of partners with no sense of direction). **X**

He can also go bald. A razor carefully taken to his little man and boys will **make his penis look bigger** by at least an inch or two. Not to mention that it'll prevent work stoppages when you have to pick the hair out of your teeth. **X**

# Get the Hole Story

Buy your own personal love stud.

47

A **tongue piercing** can work wonders for oral sex by providing extra sensation to his frenulum (that sensitive area on the underside of his wing-wang) and your clitoris (see www.safepiercing.org for info on keeping it safe when puncturing body parts). X

**Genital piercings** also improve sensation. He can get his penis pricked, but rather than wait around for him to get over his wuss attack of letting people with sharp tools down in man-land, you can get a piercing like the '**triangle**' which increases the sensitivity of your clitoris. **X**

48

49

A **nipple piercing** can turn your little bumps from something that felt OKish-nice to full-fledged erotic zones connected right to your nether regions. **X**

# Clothes Encounters

Five fashion accessories no kinkster should be seen without.

**Harness:** This contraption lets you wear a dildo like a penis. Think of the endless possibilities – you can do him, he can double do you. **X**

5 0

**Nipple clamps:** If your nips have never felt that sensitive, this will be an eye-opener. You'll feel like there's an amazing livewire connection between your nipples and your clitoris. Start small with just the tip. You can always squeeze more as you play (although you shouldn't leave them in place for more than 20 minutes or you may cause injury). **X**

**TIP:** Save money and use clothes pegs instead (wood is kinder). Test its tightness on your forefinger and thumb. If it hurts, stretch the metal spring to make it gentler.

**Vibroclips:** These are nipple clips that add an extra kick of vibration. Mmm-mmm good. **X**

**Nipple ring:** Baubles for your bumps. He'll never snub your breasts again.

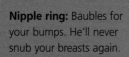

**Orgasm balls:** Your best-kept erotic secret. These small balls go clickety-clack inside your vagina all day (they are *not* worn during intercourse), keeping you on tingle alert. The best have built-in vibrators that deliver powerful, leg-trembling pulses hour after – sigh – hour. Your boss will wonder why you're so happy at work. **X**

**5**

**TIP:** Work your pelvic floor (squeeze and release your pee muscles) before slipping these in or your balls may go bouncing out at the coffee station.

**4**

# Section Three

# Playing with Props

Even the hottest couples can use some fresh, creative ways to keep their lust scorching. Luckily, there are plenty of fun accessories for raising the temperature available from sex accessory websites and stores. All you need is a little know-how and planning to get going. Get ready to lay on a red-hot, good lovin' party!

# Get the Kinks Out

Sometimes you need to push the envelope to get the sex life you want.

55

**Guaranteed orgasm booster:**
Strap on a hands-free vibe and feel your sex life soar. While you and he do the rocket jive, it'll give your – and his – lower regions a tantalizing tingle that will send you on a round-trip to the moon. **E**

# 56

**Guaranteed penis propper:** If he tends to droop, a cock ring will keep his package firmly in place. Get one with a built-in vibrator and you'll both be gyrating all night. **X**

**TIP:** Fit is everything. Go too loose and they do nothing; too tight and he'll never get soft (not as alluring as it sounds after two hours and a trip to emergency).

**Guaranteed mood swinger:** Using edible body paint, scribble naughty words all over each other's bodies. Then lick it off. Use long strokes running the length of your lover's body. **S**

**Guaranteed passion zinger:** Pick up an arousal balm and massage it on your most sensitive bits (nipples, inner thighs, genitals … you get the idea). They're spice-packed with mint or cinnamon and will give you a hot tingly sensation all over. Warning: A small amount goes a long way. **S**

**Guaranteed position pleaser:**
Give any position a little oomph by
stacking up some Liberator cushions
(www.liberatorshapes.com). These
cushions are designed to take the
hassle out of new angles and moves.
Plus you can take them anywhere, so
no more out-of-bed rug burns. **E**

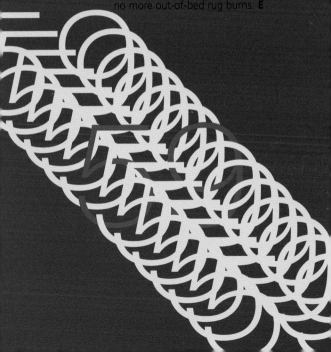

# Hot and Handy Tools

How to play with your sex toys.

## Vibrators

### 60

If your vibrator has two speeds, always **start low** so you don't jack the intensity too quickly.

### 61

When giving his popsicle a lick, rest your chin on top of a powerful vibrator to add an **incredible buzz**. X

Turn your scream machine into a sex toy for two. Slip it between your two bodies so it rests against the base of your **pleasure switch** during face2face loving. He'll be able to feel the vibrations while he's inside you. You'll both soon be pulsating with pleasure. **E**

62

Give him a tickle by stroking a happy trail with your vibrator from his lower belly to his inner thigh. Then lightly trace his **love triangle**, delicately stroking the head of his penis, moving down his shaft and gently circling his balls. Finish off by performing some **mouth magic** on him while grazing his twins and inner thighs with the vibrator. **E**

## Dildos

You'll be counting orgasms when he slips a dildo inside you while he's **licking your lips**. Especially if you look for one that's designed to rub your G-spot. **X**

64

Bring in a **stunt double**. When he needs a rest, he can fill you up with a dildo and then touch the base with a vibrator. Silicone is the most realistic material and also best for getting the vibrations to reach their target. X

**65**

## Lubes, Oils and Salves

**66**

Instead of just going in dry on your next blow job, use a gel that not only gives him a **high-pitched tickle** but also gives your tongue a **yummy razzah**. Flavours range from minty to fruity so you can have a taste test. Unfortunately, it doesn't seem to have the same effect when the roles are reversed. **E**

**67**

Make up your lips with some **vaginal lip gloss** and show him your best smile. He'll swoon over the different flavours and scents (and hopefully want to spend the whole night sampling them). **E**

**TIP:** Don't reapply the gel in an attempt to go the distance – it'll make your mouth feel like it's been to the dentist.

**68**

Smear some fruit-scented balm on your nipples and you'll want to skip dessert and head straight to bed. These **zesty creams** warm to the touch and taste heavenly. **E**

**69**

Pour massage oil directly onto your lover's skin instead of on your hand first, as you would during a regular massage. He'll ooze from the sudden feeling of the **cool massage oil** and then the warming sensation of your hand rubbing the oil in. **E**

**TIP:** Massage oil is sticky so lighter is better (the last thing you want is a thick, slick coat you can scrape off with your nails). Also, use old sheets.

# Anal Beads

Make it easy to go in or out by **lathering up** with plenty of lube. It's easier to pull out if you push down with your bottom muscles (as if going to the toilet). **X**

**70**

Don't get the **bum's rush** losing your beads. If your trinket doesn't have a ring or handle on the end, leave one or two beads outside the opening so you can pull them out. **X**

71

**Timing is everything**. Send your lover into a tailspin by s-l-o-w-l-y pulling the beads out during orgasm (they'll have to let you know when blast-off is, so you can start pulling). **X**

72

# On the Menu

Put a little kink in your sex diet.

Have a feeding frenzy. Make an **edible passion shopping list** and then send your lover to pick up the booty. Suggestions: cake icing tubes to write on each other with, mints or pop rocks to tuck into your mouth for effervescent oral sex, ice cream to dab on and lick off hot bits, donuts to ring around his erect penis and nibble off, and Champagne for lapping out of your concave places. **S**

**TIP:** Chocolate does not wash off skin easily and leaves embarrassing brown streaks.

For chocolate lovers: When his penis is soft, run an ice cube over it and then cover it with **chocolate syrup** that hardens (available at any supermarket). Just make sure you suck instead of bite! **S**

# Household Goodies

Skip the toy store – here are nine things you have around the house to push your sex life to the edge.

**75**

A **silk scarf** can double up as a blindfold or an impromptu hand and leg truss so you can have your wicked way. **S**

**76**

A **ruler** or **flat-headed hairbrush** will transform you into the impatient teacher ready to discipline a disobedient student (or vice versa). **X**

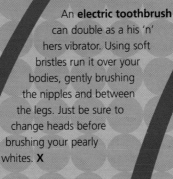

An **electric toothbrush** can double as a his 'n' hers vibrator. Using soft bristles run it over your bodies, gently brushing the nipples and between the legs. Just be sure to change heads before brushing your pearly whites. **X**

Have a dust up with a **feather duster** – you can use it to apply honey dust or icing sugar to various body parts and then lick off your dirty work. **S**

Or pluck out just **one feather** to tickle your lover's bottom hole. **X**

Wrapping **sheer, silky stockings** around your hands like gloves will turn your hand 'job' into a pleasure. It's easier on you than using a dry hand and the sensuous fabric will make him crumple. **S**

**81**

Make an impromptu cockring by scrunching a **fabric hairband** around his penis base (not *too* tightly). It'll keep him in a state of suspended lust and the fabric will give a pleasure nudge to your love centre. **E**

Light an **unscented, white candle** (perfumes, colourings and beeswax all make the candle burn hotter) and tilt it above your lover's body to allow a single drop of hot wax to land on the skin at a time. For extreme thrills, alternate between hot wax and ice and slip on a **blindfold** so everything comes as a sexy shock. **X**

**82**

**TIP:** If you're planning below-the-belt drippings, shave first or die.

Set a **camera** on self-time to take sneaky snaps of you two getting it on. If it's digital, you can download the pics to your computer and even alter the images to make your own private x-rated blog paradise. **X**

83

# Section Four

# Tease Please

The fun starts here. You don't have to be into S&M to experience the pure erotic thrill that comes from playing tie-up games with your lover. Flexing your dominatrix muscles and calling the foreplay shots is a powerful turn-on. On the other hand, simply be a prisoner of your lover's lust and let them have their wicked way with you.

Don't worry. You won't need special equipment to get started (that's for later!). Just pack your imagination and the desire to romp rough. But remember: Sex, no matter how wild, is supposed to be about loving it up – not drawing blood!

# How to Be the Boss in the Bedroom

Don't be skittish about telling your lover exactly what you want.

# 84

Play **Lover, May I?**. The rule of the game: No touching without asking, 'May I touch/lick/suck/bang your...' (insert favourite bit here). Naming the parts means you'll be forced to mouth off like porn stars. You can add a dom tone by establishing your **chick-in-charge** position and occasionally denying him access. **S**

Practise **verbal bondage** by telling him to act like a statue. He holds his hands up, each fingertip touching the opposite fingertip. Put a penny between each pair of fingertips so he's holding five pennies. Now order him not to let a single one drop, on pain of punishment (such as he has to be your **sex slave** for one day) and then go to work ravishing him.

**TIP:** This works best on a hard floor so you can hear the coin drop – which it definitely will. **E**

85

Don't give him a chance to think – straddle him, pull his head back with a tug of his hair and just take him. Use **tough-love techniques** like naughty ear and neck nips, pushing your fingertips deep into the fleshiest part of his buttocks while he thrusts, pulling his face to your breasts as you hit your passion peak. He'll be delighted with your diva moves. **E**

Swap roles and have him put on the **bad-boy persona**. Say you want him to take you on the rough side. His script: To pounce and hold you down, then breathe in your ear how hot he is (his talk should be part Romeo, part porno). Sex up the scenario by pretending to push him away, you **damsel in desire**! **E**

**8**

Lie back on the bed with your arms outstretched and purr, **'Do whatever you want with me.' S**

**8**

**9**

Always **cuddle** after. S

# See No Evil

Give new meaning to the phrase, 'love is blind'.

Once you've got your man blind, treat him to a slew of new sensations: gently nibble him, trail your **hardened tongue** over his body, tickle him with your fingers, swish your hair over his bits. He'll have no idea where you'll strike next. At the crucial moment, climb on top, hold his face and make him stare right into your eyes as you **ride him to oblivion**. E

**TIP:** Start low-key and use your hands instead of a blindfold to cover his eyes.

91

Tantalize him by slipping a scarf over his orbs and teasing him any way you desire. You're in **total control** of his pleasure, so pull out the stops by stimulating him with sensual props (see Section 3 for ideas). Mix up your touch to keep his **temperature** high. E

**TIP:** Don't forget to take a turn behind the veil so he can have fun ordering up your moans and groans.

92

Have a fox hunt. You both get naked but one of you wears a blindfold (a scarf will do). The other hides. The **masked lover** gets on hands and knees (to avoid tripping or bumping into things) and has to find the other. The hider can pop up out of nowhere, only to disappear in the next instant. **Tally-ho! E**

# Get Fit-to-Be-Tied

How to tie one on and feel no pain.

When you're ready to be bound
for love, don't reach for the **handcuffs**
unless they're specially made for sex play
(fur-lined, for example). The metal versions
are more likely to bruise your wrists or – worse
– break mid-play. The beginner's best is nylon
because they open easily, and are affordable
and comfy to wear. DIYers can use
scarves, bandanas, stockings,
a tie or cotton rope.

**TIP:** Always tie
them loosely so you
can get out easily
in a pinch.

**94**

If your bed has
no posts, you can wrap
ropes around the legs of the bed
and **spread-eagle your lover**. Or tie
his wrists behind his back and then
to his waist. **X**

Have him **tie your hands and feet** together
and then set you up on your elbows and
knees. He then comes from behind to
worship you mercilessly while you
love every minute of it. **X**

95

Tie him to a chair and then do a **striptease** followed by a **lap dance** (see tip 32 for how-to). **E**

**96**

Tickling is **terrific torture** that's especially good if he's all tied up with nowhere to go. Run a feather up and down his body until he begs for mercy. **S**

**TIP:** When he returns the favour, you may discover you're one of the few lucky women who can get tickled to orgasm.

**97**

One tormenting trick he can try on you: He ties you spread-eagled to the bed and rests a vibrator on your push button. While he plays with your breasts, you'll be **writhing like a disco dancer** trying to get the buzz exactly where you want it. **X**

# Spank Amateurs

It's swattin' time.

Next time you're smack bang in the heat of things, whisper to your partner that you've been bad and you need a spanking. Add a little **bottom squirming** to emphasize your point. **E**

If you plan to be in charge of the smackdown, make sure he knows. Wear **black thigh-high boots** and a **naughty teddy** to set the mood and then tell him he's been misbehaving and needs to be punished. **X**

Get your lover in **spanking position**. The classic pose for her is bent over his knee with her bottom up for a good licking. If he's on the receiving end, he should lean against a waist-high object (table, bed, car) that'll brace him against her thumps.

**Spank it like a pro.** Your lover's bottom is not your boss's face, so keep your everyday aggressions out of the bedroom. **Start by rubbing** (you can rub one or both cheeks, but only smack one cheek at a time). Don't worry, before you know it, they'll turn the other cheek. After you smack it, rub the area a little bit, not only to soften the blow, but also to show that it was an affectionate butt whooping.

**Hit the bull's-eye.** The hind end's sweet spot is the well-padded bit where cheek meets the thigh. Spank close to the genitals and they'll indirectly get stimulated, sending your sugarbaby into sweet oblivion. **E**

Keep the rhythm. The winning beat: two light smacks, one slightly harder, then three light smacks and one hard one, and repeat. This build-up will deem you **Spank Master**. **E**

End with a bang. Spanking sessions end when the one on the receiving end cries, 'Uncle'. Ask, **'Will you be good now?'** If they agree, lay off, kick back, and let them show you exactly how good. **E**

# Section Five

# Pushing the Limits

Same time, same place, same position?
Some fun and games can shake you
out of your ho-hum routine.

Most of these tips take some preparation.
But working a kinky act is never a quickie,
which is why doing it makes you pant with
lust. Deciding what secret desire you want
to play out, stocking up on the equipment
and planning the scene together are all part
of the buzz. So shelve your inhibitions
and get ready to vice things up with
these sextreme suggestions.

# Bottom's Up

The ins and outs of rear-ending in the bedroom.

106

It's not a vagina; it doesn't secrete fluid. Unless you want to see your lover leap up and dig their nails into the ceiling, **grease up**. Silicone lubes (versus glycerine ones like K-Y and some versions of Wet and Astroglide) are slick and slidey and stay that way longer.

For obvious reasons, it's a good idea for the partner on the receiving end to take a trip to the toilet (and possibly the shower for a **soapy wash**) before anything gets started.

107

You don't have to go for a deep plunge. The highest concentration of nerve endings is around the anal opening itself so just inch your finger or tongue in for a quick **skinny dip** while playing at the other end. **E**

The key is re-lax-ation. Start off with a long, **warm bath**, or better yet, give your lover a few **teeth-numbing**, stupefying orgasms before you head 'round back. **S**

109

If you do decide to do a full bottom bungee jump, follow these four steps for a smooth dive.

- **Get cheeky.** Don't lunge straight for the hole. Spreading and softly squeezing and rubbing your lover's derrière will put them in a relaxed, receptive mood. **S**

- **Test the waters** with one, then two (well-lubed) fingers before you let little Johnny jump in. Work your way up very gradually, gently stroking the region right around the opening, then pushing gently at the centre but not actually penetrating. **E**

- **Get into position** – puppy style is easiest for newbies. **E**

**TIP:** Hopping on top means you can call the shots but it tends to tighten your butt muscles, making penetration tougher.

- Once the head of the penis is in, **stop and relax** for a couple minutes, to get used to the sensation.

Turn him into a love fool by **poking his prostate** (on the rectal wall on the side toward his genitals). **Lick his lollipop** at the same time and watch him drool. **X**

**1½**

**2**

Try a little **rim around the rosie** with your tongue. Make your tongue flat and hard for the most **yum-gasmic** sensation. **X**

**Toy with
your bottom.**
Use a small dildo
or vibrator specifically
made for anal insertion
(they're flared so won't get
sucked in and lost in your no-
man's land) or **butt plug** (a small
flared stopper that's inserted and
sometimes
left in the
bottom) or
anal beads (think cheap
plastic necklace – see tips 70–2).

Use lots of **hands-on techniques**. While making a pass
at the back door, work in a double play by slipping your
other hand around the front end. He can use fingers or
a vibrator on her orgasm lever or navigate his way down
her vaginal canal, bumping along the bottom wall to
buoy up the **pleasure waves** while she can pull on his
boys or give his wood a jiggle. **X**

# Fantasy Island

How to make your dreams come true.

Make sharing time easier when it comes to your erotic whimsies. Scribble your **top three fantasies** on a piece of paper and number them from one to six. Toss a die and pick whichever number comes up with the promise you'll act it out. **E**

Act out an **orgy à deux**.
Close your eyes or use
blindfolds and work all your
digits and tongues at the same
time: play with nipples while
using your mouth down below;
**slide a dildo** in from behind
while using a vibe mitt in front.
It'll feel like a gangbuster. **S**

If the thought – but not the reality – of adding another
girl to your love dance makes you liquefy, arrange to
get an at-home rub-down while he watches. You'll get
warmed up with a **mah-vellous massage** and plenty
of material to fire your engines later. **E**

# Get into the Role

Throw your own private fancy dress party.

Five things to put in your closet right now: **X**

| HER | HIM |
|---|---|
| **Corset** | **Pirate outfit** |
| **Any uniform** (nurse, maid) | **Any uniform** (cop, firefighter) |
| **Catsuit** (fishnet, latex, silky material) | **Leather trousers** |
| **Cheerleader** | **Football player** |
| **Vamp** (think cleavage and tight) | **Male stripper** (think thong) |

118

Role-playing is a sexcellent way to add **risky razzle-dazzle** to your romps. Some good first-time scenes: **X**

### Doctor/patient
('It's time for your breast exam')

### Highway patrolman/motorist
('Step out of the car, please')

### Mechanic/customer
('How can I service you?')

### Hooker/john
(You figure it out)

### Teacher/student
('You need extra homework')

# Porn to be Wild

Try these and you'll end up having sex so hot that the porn will look tame in comparison.

Skip the down-and-dirty porno movies that men tend to jive to and go for more sensual and **mind-teasing films** that'll make your vagina sing (Vivid Video and Femme productions are female-friendly). Then pick your favourite scenes to re-enact for real. **E**

**Four movie scenes to steal from:**

***Basic Instinct*:**
Tie his hands to the bedposts and ride him like a soldier.

***Wild Orchid*:** Wear a mask while he plays a sexy stranger who seduces you.

**Direct your own porno shoot** for your viewing pleasure. Strategies for charging up the action (while keeping those extra ten pounds film adds off): use candles, keep some clothes on, film outside the bedroom, zoom in on your face rather than your body parts, **turn up the heat** to avoid goosebumps. **X**

**TIP:** You keep the evidence.

*Body of Evidence*: Indulge in a clothes-ripping, hair-pulling, tied-up, hot-candle wax moment.

*9½ Weeks*: Oh, where to begin? Perhaps the blindfolded fridge raid.

# One Step Beyond

Everything else is for rookies – for bona-fide kink cred…

## TRY:

**Tripling up:**
Double up on your pleasure, double up on your fun.

**Cyber sex:**
Commitment-free-anything-goes-fantasy sex online – do it with strangers or your lover. And you don't even have to dress for the occasion.

**Clubbing:**
Experience the thrill of peeping into someone else's deviant fun.

**Swinging:**
Explore your fantasies in a fairly safe environment.

## 123456

# MAKE IT SIN-SATIONAL

Go to a **high-end spot** or you may find yourself in a love nest filled with one-handed warriors. **X**

There is a swing group for **every urge** so be clear on the action before paying your initiation fee. **X**

The more descriptive you can be, the better. And **type carefully** (no one wants to read 'stick your clock in me' at the brink of melt-down. **X**

Don't pay too much attention to the **third wheel** or you may end up solo. **X**

## Sex Toys

**Ann Summers:** www.annsummers.com

**Blowfish:** www.blowfish.com

**Good Vibrations:** www.goodvibrations.com

**LoveHoney:** www.lovehoney.co.uk

**Sh!:** www.sh-womenstore.com

## Dress Up

**Sexy outfits galore:** www.bionictonic.co.uk/sex toys/thongs.html

**Stiletto heaven:** http://007stilettoshoes.safeshopper.com

**More stiletto heaven:** www.amberssecrets.com

**UK Consumer Information Website on piercing precautions:**
www.consumereducation.org.uk/features/piercings.htm

**USA Association of Professional Piercers:** 888–515–4APP,
www.safepiercing.org

## Swinging

**One of largest swinging groups in the USA:** www.nasca.com

**Top swinging sites worldwide:** www.oast.com/adult/topsites/1

## Acknowledgements

Mega thanks (and amazement) to everyone on my IM list and
especially to those strangers who brazenly contributed their tips
and experiences to this book. Also special thanks to Lisa Dyer,
whose ever-wise and patient input has proved invaluable.